Edmund K Alden

The world's Representative Assemblies of Today

A Study in Comparative Legislation

Edmund K Alden

The world's Representative Assemblies of Today
A Study in Comparative Legislation

ISBN/EAN: 9783744725224

Printed in Europe, USA, Canada, Australia, Japan

Cover: Foto ©ninafisch / pixelio.de

More available books at **www.hansebooks.com**

JOHNS HOPKINS UNIVERSITY STUDIES

IN

HISTORICAL AND POLITICAL SCIENCE

HERBERT B. ADAMS, Editor

History is past Politics and Politics present History.—*Freeman*

ELEVENTH SERIES

II

THE WORLD'S REPRESENTATIVE ASSEMBLIES OF TO-DAY

A STUDY IN COMPARATIVE LEGISLATION

BY EDMUND K. ALDEN

BALTIMORE

THE JOHNS HOPKINS PRESS

PUBLISHED MONTHLY

February, 1893

PREFACE.

A few words on the arrangement of the matter in the following monograph may not be irrelevant. The placing of the Table of Assemblies at the end is intended to facilitate reference. Such a table was also necessary to illustrate the preceding statements, as the prescribed limits precluded a seriatim treatment of the different legislative bodies. The same limitations of space have necessarily excluded much that would enhance the value and interest of such a table, as, for example, the minutiæ of qualifications for electors and members.

The statements made are based in all cases on the latest available sources. As information on some topics has been tendered to me personally, I take this opportunity of expressing my thanks to those who have in this way contributed to the work.

EDMUND K. ALDEN.

PACKER COLLEGIATE INSTITUTE,
    BROOKLYN, N. Y., *January* 3, 1893.

SYNOPSIS.

LIMITS OF THE SUBJECT.—GENERAL DIVISION INTO CONGRESSES AND PARLIAMENTS.—NOMENCLATURE.

COMMENTS ON THE ELECTORATE :
Its Relation to the Population ; Direct and Indirect Election.

ON THE COMPOSITION OF THE HOUSES :
Unicameral and Bicameral Systems.
Qualifications of Members.
Size of the Chambers.
Relative Importance of the Houses.
Distribution of Members.
Apportionment.
Terms of Service.
Re-election.

ON THE POWERS OF LEGISLATIVE BODIES :
The Initiative in Legislation.
Relations to the Executive.
Constitutional Restrictions.

ON PROCEDURE :
Officers.
Rules.
Committees.
Various Forms.

ON PARLIAMENTARY MANNERS.

ON PERSONALITY OF MEMBERS.

ON LOCAL ASSEMBLIES.

ON THE REFERENDUM AND THE INITIATIVE.

RECAPITULATION.

TABLE OF THE LARGER REPRESENTATIVE ASSEMBLIES.

THE WORLD'S REPRESENTATIVE ASSEMBLIES OF TO-DAY.

A STUDY IN COMPARATIVE LEGISLATION.

The great development of popular government has led to diversified and exhaustive studies on the subject. Historical literature has been enriched by countless manuals of politics and by treatises of profound learning on the theory and practice of ruling. But we look almost in vain for an *aperçu* or bird's-eye view of all the legislative bodies of the present. The plan of this monograph is foreshadowed in its title; it does not claim to trace the genesis and evolution of existing assemblies, nor—deeply interesting and informing as the task would be—can the labor of a detailed analysis and commentary on all modern legislatures fall within its scope. It seeks rather to set in array the principal phenomena of such assemblies, and from the data furnished to draw the more striking and essential lessons.

An accepted classification of legislatures is that of Congresses and Parliaments, whose fundamental distinction lies in the presence in a Parliament of an executive or ministry chosen wholly or mainly from its own numbers. The Old World is the home of the Parliament, as the New World is of the Congress. The Parliament is the older form, for, as Sir Henry Maine says, "The American Constitution is distinctively English,"[1] and again, "There is no doubt that the modern popular government of our day is of purely English origin."[2] The example of the British Parliament was followed by France, Spain, Portugal, and the Netherlands, in the great constitution-forming epoch after the fall

---

[1] Maine, *Popular Government*, 11. [2] *Ib.* 8.

of Napoleon, and more tardily by Italy, Germany, Austria-Hungary, and others; and it is the prevalent form in Great Britain's leading colonies. While she furnished the standard type for parliamentary government, her stalwart offspring supplied the model for Congresses.

The guiding principle is that the administration—the "government"—must be in sympathy, politically, with the popular house. This is the case both in lands with an aristocratic upper house, and in countries like France, where the political complexion of the Senate no longer affects the administration.[1]

Marked deviations from the English type occur. In France, for instance, ministerial responsibility is, to insular views, in a more embryonic stage; the successor of a defeated ministry frequently contains prominent members of its predecessor, and depends for support partly on the adherents of this ministry. The alignment of party groups in the Parliaments of the Continent, their combinations and readjustments, seem more erratic than political changes in the British bodies. So recent is the *régime* of the Reichstag in Germany that the significance of an adverse majority vote is ill defined. But there is a family resemblance discernible as we follow the proceedings of the European bodies, except in countries with a burlesque popular government.[2]

When we consider the United States Congress we are, in more senses than one, in another world. That authoritative writer on "Congressional Government," Prof. Woodrow Wilson, says: "The parliamentary debates are interesting, and ours are not. . . In the British House of Commons the functions of our Standing Committees are all concentrated in the hands of the Ministry. Every important discussion is an arraignment of the Ministry by the Oppo-

---

[1] Burgess, *Political Science*, II., 26.
[2] The present rule in Bulgaria is happily characterized by F. Hopkinson Smith as a government of *opéra bouffe*.

sition. And every important vote is a party defeat and a party triumph."[1]

On the other hand we may set the opinion of an equally close observer: " I must not be understood as advocating the European plan as preferable for this country. The evils that inevitably flow from any fundamental change in the institutions of a country are apt to be much more serious than the evils which the change is intended to remove. Political government is like a plant; a little watering and pruning do very well for it, but the less its roots are fooled with the better. In the American system of government the independence of the executive department, with reference to the legislative, is fundamental, and on the whole it is eminently desirable."[2]

The nomenclature presents some interesting features. Congress is the name in the New World;[3] Senate is the word for the upper chamber, House of Representatives or Chamber of Representatives for the lower. In the separate States of the Union, Legislature or General Assembly is the usual term for the whole body; but the two old States of Massachusetts and New Hampshire still preserve the name of General Court, while a few Western States have a Legislative Assembly. The States unanimously call their upper house the Senate; the lower body is generally termed House of Representatives; but New York and a few Western States speak of their Assembly, New Jersey of the General Assembly, Maryland and the two Virginias of the House of Delegates.

Abroad, Parliament, or some word equivalent to Diet, is commonly used for the law-making body, and the native names of Storthing, Cortes, Sobranje, Skupshtina, and Boulé, are also encountered. The Portuguese House of Peers, the Prussian, Austrian, and British House of Lords, the Hun-

---

[1] Wilson, *Congressional Government*, 94.
[2] Fiske, *Civil Government*, 169.
[3] But Parliament is used in Uruguay.

garian House of Magnates, proclaim their character; while for the lower house we find that Chamber of Deputies is a common form.

The larger British colonies naturally copy the example of the mother country, as the Cape, Victorian, or Canadian Parliament; but we find that Legislative Council is the almost universal name for the upper house in British colonial bodies; the nomenclature of their lower houses is varied.

In considering the important topic of the electorate of a country, we notice, first, the relation of this electorate to the whole population. Universal suffrage, it is needless to say, obtains in the United States, though Delaware still adheres to a tax qualification in State Senate elections. On the American continent universal suffrage, on the whole, prevails, but the exceptions are numerous. In Canada a property qualification exists. In Mexico the electorate comprises " all respectable male adults "—a somewhat elastic term. Costa Rica limits the suffrage to " those able to live respectably "—a rule that would, if strictly enforced, result, in many localities, in the establishment of a close oligarchy. Ecuador makes a religious test: Roman Catholic adults, able to read and write. Chili requires a property or income qualification. Brazil presents a novel feature, in that it disfranchises soldiers and members of certain monastic orders. The humor of a rather dry subject is furnished by Hayti, which enacts the requirement that her citizens should " have some vocation."

Since the Act of 1884, the British electorate is increased to include about one-sixth of the population (one-fourth to nine-fortieths being about the normal ratio). Some peculiar restrictions are observed in the colonial bodies. For example, in the Victorian Parliament, while the lower house is elected by general suffrage, the Legislative Council is chosen by electors with a property qualification; but clergymen, lawyers, medical practitioners, army and navy officers, and graduates of a British university are electors *per se*, so that a premium is placed on learning. The same respect to education is shown in Tasmania; in general the Australian colonies are fond of a property or income qualification, and this is true of several other British possessions.

Those great bodies, the German Reichstag and French Chamber of Deputies, are chosen by general suffrage; but these cases are exceptional. The restrictions are many and diversified. For the Portuguese lower house the requirements are so comparatively insignificant that the electorate embraces one-fifth of the population; the stipulations in Italy limit the electorate for the lower house to one-tenth of the inhabitants, and attendance at the voting-urns in 1892[1] was fifty per cent. of the electorate; in the Netherlands the ratio is one-fifteenth; in Spain, Denmark, Norway, and Sweden, about one-seventeenth. In the several German States the electorate for the local Landtags is restricted in less than half the number (including, however, Bavaria). For relics of the feudal system we must go to Mecklenburg, where no body exists to represent the people at large. Neither the Austrian and Hungarian bodies, nor the Landtags of the crown lands, are chosen by general suffrage. Bulgaria and Greece—recent additions to the household of nations—allow manhood suffrage. Switzerland has general suffrage for its National Council, but the cantons differ considerably in electoral requirements regarding the cantonal legislatures. To relieve the tedium of these details, we may note an electoral provision in Montenegro, where half of the members of the nominal State Council are elected by citizens able to bear arms,—a provision which in that warlike little principality must include nearly everybody outside of cradles.

While property and income qualifications are the common forms of restriction, various others are found. Japan disfranchises priests; the Orange Free State draws the color line in its Volksraed; Italy favors learned men, as members of academies. Both Denmark and Norway exclude house-

---

[1] *Nation*, Dec. 8, 1892.

hold servants. The free cities of Germany are quite aristocratic in their provisions, and favor the taxpayers and
merchants. Hungary exempts certain professional and
learned classes—chemists, engineers, etc.—from the small
income or real estate qualification, and extends this exemp-
tion to an artisan having a single workman under him.[1]

Direct election is the preferred form, though there are
some notable exceptions. These include Costa Rica, Peru,
and some small German States; part of the Austrian
Abgeordnetenhaus is chosen in this way, and so are, in
part, the Austrian Landtags. Rumania, too, has electoral
colleges. But perhaps the most noteworthy instance of
indirect election is that for the Prussian Chamber of
Deputies. The electors, in the first instance, are classed in
three groups, favoring the highest payers of direct taxes, by
an arrangement which somewhat reminds one of the old
Roman centuries and classes.

The bicameral system has met the approval of most of
the leading political writers,[2] and is realized in practice by
the legislatures of the principal countries. Legislative bodies
with a single chamber are common in cities, in departmental,
provincial, and county councils. Many of the smaller American cities and some of the larger[3] have a council of one
chamber. But every[4] American State legislature has two
houses. The unicameral bodies fall into three or four
main groups: the Parliaments of the minor States of south-
eastern Europe, Servia, Bulgaria, and Greece; the Congresses of the States of Central America, Nicaragua ex-
cepted, compose another group; the Landtags of the
Austrian crown lands are one-chambered, and so are nearly
all the Diets of the minor German States, excepting those
of the free cities.

---

[1] Victor Tissot, *Unknown Hungary*, I., 134.
[2] Bagehot is a notable exception.
[3] *E. g.*, New York, San Francisco, Brooklyn.
[4] Pennsylvania was formerly an exception.

A qualification of members is usually required, on the lines of age, as in the United States and generally, or of property, as is usually the case in Europe and the British possessions; or certain classes may be non-eligible: Brazil objects to clergy, ministers of state, and military officers in its lower house. The French Senate rules out generals and admirals in active service. Victoria bars out clergymen, and South Australia excludes both clergymen and judges. Italy also debars priests from its lower house. In the Portuguese Chamber, members, if they belong to the learned professions, are not subjected to the property qualification. Hungary has a provision suggestive of reflection. It declares non-eligible members of financial societies having relations with the State, and administrators of subsidized railroads.[1] The South African Republic (Transvaal), besides other qualifications, requires candidates for the Volksraed to be members of a Protestant church,—a stipulation which calls up to Americans a reminiscence of Puritan New England in colonial times.

In the composition of the two houses, wherever there is a difference, the divergence is striking. If an age limit is required, that for the upper house is considerably greater. If property qualification is the test, the member of the upper house is rated far higher. So it is with length of residence and with length of terms of service. Of the forty-four individual States of the American Union, only thirteen have equal terms for the two houses; the States frequently allot either four years for the Senate and two years for the lower house, or two years and one year respectively. Brazil, Sweden, and Hawaii, like the United States, give to the upper house thrice the term of service assigned to the lower.

A comparison of the relative size of the two houses is interesting. The upper is, with hardly an exception, the smaller. In some cases—notably in Europe—the disparity is not great. The House of Lords numbers 559 and the

---

[1] *Cf.* V. Tissot, *Unknown Hungary*, II., 134.

Commons 670; the two chambers of the Spanish Cortes are nearly equal,—not far from 400. The upper body in the Swedish and Italian Parliaments is not greatly inferior to the lower in point of numbers; and the Hungarian House of Magnates actually counts a few more than the popular branch; while the new Japanese Parliament preserves almost a parity. But the ratio is generally large. In most of the American States the Senate is one-half to one-third the size of the popular body. In New York, Pennsylvania, and Georgia the ratio is 1 : 4, in Massachusetts 1 : 6, in Vermont 1 : 8, in Connecticut 1 : 12, in New Hampshire 1 : 15, and in Delaware 1 : 22. Delaware has the smallest legislative body of the States,—a Senate of 9.

On the question of size it would appear that when a certain point—perhaps about 250 or 300—is passed, the working qualities of the legislature are impaired. The American House of Representatives has steadily grown, and its present number, 356, seems to many too large for a business body. The old States of New Hampshire, Massachusetts, Connecticut, and Vermont show the largest houses, and all reach or surpass 240. The largest State, New York, has a Senate of only 32 and a lower house of only 128. Turning to the Old World, we find in the House of Commons the largest legislative body, 670; but the French Chamber is not far behind with 584 members. The lower houses of all the great European powers are equal or far superior in numbers to our House at Washington. It is to be noted that representative bodies of a temporary character are still more unwieldy. Thus the national conventions have double the membership of both houses of Congress together. The annual convention of the Massachusetts Republicans has over 1000 members. Bulgaria has a Great Sobranje, convened on extraordinary occasions, and this is just twice the size of the Sobranje proper, and there is a similar extraordinary assembly in Servia.

As to the relative importance of the houses, the close hold which, in a democratic age, the lower house has on the people, the constitutional lead which it so generally maintains in financial and revenue affairs give it an undoubted pre-eminence.   In view of the great powers of the United States Senate in the matters of treaties and confirmations of appointments, one is tempted to consider it an exception to the rule. But it is the Chamber of Deputies whose proceedings we follow, not the French Senate; the Austrian Abgeordnetenhaus, not the Herrenhaus. The House of Lords concerns us little compared with its mighty confrère. Says Sir Henry Maine on this point: "We are drifting towards . . . a single Assembly; it will be a theoretically all-powerful Convention, governed by a practically all-powerful secret Committee of Public Safety."[1]

The United States Senate is by general consent[2] one of the most powerful organizations in the world.   Besides the privilege of initiating any bills except those for revenue, and of amending, concurring in or rejecting the House bills, it confirms or vetoes many of the most important appointments by the President, such as the nominees to diplomatic and consular missions, judges (including those of the Supreme Court), various notable officers in the civil service; nominally, too, it confirms or rejects the members of the Cabinet, although this latter privilege is practically a dead letter, even when, as is often the case, the President and the Senate majority belong to antagonistic parties.   In addition, the Senate's assent is necessary for the validity of all treaties. The "Upper House," by reason of its mode of election and smaller size, is less sensitive to changes of public opinion than the House of Representatives.

The principles involved in the terms *scrutin de liste* and congressman-at-large call for some comment.   The French system of voting for the half-dozen deputies of a department on a "general ticket" has, after some fluctuations, since 1889 been supplanted by the district method of

---

[1] Maine, *Popular Government*, 126.
[2] *E. g., cf.* Maine, *Popular Government*, 226.

scrutin d'arrondissement. A few cases of *scrutin de liste* occur elsewhere. On the contrasting policies of choosing representatives at large or by districts, or rather of exacting or not exacting a residence in the district represented, we may quote Bryce. In an address at the Johns Hopkins Historical Seminary[1] he earnestly expressed the view—afterwards elaborated in his "American Commonwealth"—that the practice of restricting candidates to residents of the district is a cardinal error of the American system. It can readily be seen how this arrangement frequently keeps well-equipped lawmakers out of the Congress or Legislature. On the other hand, as the representative is supposed to serve primarily a district, and not the State or nation, it may well be urged that he should have that familiarity with the district's needs which residence alone could give. So strong is the American prejudice on the matter that instances of nonresidence in the district very rarely occur; when an outside candidate appears, the cry of " carpet-bagger " is likely to be raised, and with effect.[2]

Where, as in an upper house, members are chosen without regard to districts, some respect to geographical distribution is often shown. To refer again to an American example: if one United States Senator from a given State is identified through residence or interests with the northern or western part of that State, the other will be taken from the southern or eastern portion. This principle is indeed often violated, and has little hold in some States; but in Maryland one of the Senators is invariably chosen from the Eastern Shore,—a region which contains one-fifth of the population of that commonwealth.

An attempt to realize a just apportionment is now made in the British House of Commons. No borough with a population under 10,000 has a representative. Boroughs

---

[1] 1883.

[2] *E. g.*, in the Sixth Massachusetts District, 1890 and 1892, Everett *vs.* Lodge.

of between 10,000 and 50,000 have one each; of between 50,000 and 165,000 two each. Boroughs of over 165,000 have one additional member for each 50,000 to 60,000.

The apportionment in France, in the Chamber of Deputies, is reasonably equitable, in the ratio of 1 : 70,000 inhabitants. In the German Reichstag it is very unequal: some members represent less than 12,000 inhabitants; others, over 160,000. No attempt at apportionment is made in the Landtags of the, Austrian crown lands.

We may say in general that attempts to realize a fair apportionment for the lower chamber at least are in vogue, and the ratio of a member to the number of inhabitants is generally least in the least populous countries. Thus the United States shows the large ratio of 1 : 173,000; Italy, 1 : 57,000; France, 1 : 70,000; while Paraguay has 1 : 6000, and Uruguay 1 : 3000.

As the States of the American Union vary greatly in population, the disproportionate representation of the minor States—notable even at the adoption of the Constitution— has become excessive. In Nevada 21,000 persons are represented by a United States Senator; in New York nearly 3,000,000, a ratio of 1 : 140; these are the extremes. In Wyoming and Idaho a Senator's constituency is 30,000 to 40,000; in Pennsylvania, Ohio, and Illinois it is 2,000,000 to 3,000,000.

Each representative has a constituency of approximately 173,000 persons. This theoretical attempt at comparative equality of representation is in practice considerably modified; yet the distribution is fairer than that in the British House of Commons, in the lower houses of many Continental countries, and in the Assemblies of many of the individual States. Several causes combine to retard the approach to an ideal apportionment. Three States have a population far less than the standard of representation, yet each is entitled to a member. In others the arrangement into districts is unequal, or it becomes so through the unequal development of different sections. In some States, for local reasons, nearly the whole electorate takes part in choosing a Congressman; in others perhaps one-half or less than one-half of the voters exercise their rights. Moreover, the system of gerrymandering often works unjustly, separating, for political purposes, regions contiguous and related in interests.

I quote a few cases of disproportionate representation in Congressional districts:[1] Population of the Second Californian District, 150,571; of the Sixth, 315,094. Connecticut showed in the Third District 121,792; in the Second, 248,582. Minnesota showed 171,271 in the First, and 414,635 in the Fourth. Coming nearer home, in New York the Sixth[2] District had 107,844, and the Thirteenth[3] had 312,404. The evil has no local home. The Third Pennsylvania District had 129,764, and the next, the Fourth, had 309,086.

The distribution of seats in State legislatures is frequently uneven. New York presents some instances of this; in Wisconsin, by a recent gerrymander (reversed, however, by the Supreme Court), while the basis of population for a member in the Assembly is 16,868, four districts exhibit these figures: 6823, 7923, 16,868 and 25,143.[4] But the most glaring cases of rotten boroughs occur in New England, in Vermont,[5] and notably in Connecticut; in this unfortunate State, to quote from a recent publicist,[6] there would be found in the lower house " one town with a population of 86,045 equalized with another town having a population of but 431; and as to the State Senate, a district which at the Presidential election of 1888 cast 17,649 votes equalized with another district casting but 2585 votes." We are reminded of Old Sarum.

---

[1] *Congressional Directory*, 1891.
[2] In New York City. [3] *Ibid.*
[4] New York *Evening Post*, Dec. 1891.
[5] H. White, *Fortnightly Review*, 32 : 506.
[6] *The Nation*, Dec. 17, 1891.

There are in the upper house some instances of attempted apportionment with a view to population. But where the federal system of government prevails, the individuality of the component parts has been jealously guarded. Compare the equal representation of the States in the Senate, in the American Union, with that of the Cantons in the Swiss Council of States.

Few bodies have longer terms of existence than six years. The model furnished by the United States Senate was followed by some countries further south, though the Argentine Republic and Brazil elect Senators for the extraordinarily long term of nine years. This is also the term of the First Chamber in the Netherlands. A maximum limit (infrequently reached) within which time the Chamber may be dissolved, of seven, five years, etc., is seen in the House of Commons,[1] Italian Chamber, and many others. In general, our Eastern and older States cling to short terms; the newer and Western States prescribe longer periods. The term in the Senate is frequently double that of the lower house in the States. Four and two years respectively is the combination now in use in twenty-seven out of the forty-four States. One State—Mississippi—assigns four years to each house.

No generalization can be made involving a comparison of short or long terms of service and political freedom or repression in the respective countries.

In regard to re-election of members, the best examples of long service are to be found in the House of Commons. Instances of ten and fifteen years' service are common; twenty or thirty years are not rare. Gladstone's case is often quoted; a continuous service—except a short intermission in 1846-47—from December, 1832, to the present time; but remarkable as that is, it does not greatly exceed some other records.[2] The parliamentary careers of Continental leaders

---

[1] Of twenty-three Parliaments in this century, only three have passed the six-year limit.

[2] *E. g.*, Palmerston, Russell.

are frequently long. The prominent men in the Assemblies of France, Spain, and Italy, for example, have been re-elected again and again. In the United States Senate re-election is common. Not a few Senators are a second time re-elected, and there are some instances of service like the uninterrupted thirty years of Benton, the twenty-three years of Sumner, or the twenty-eight years of Sherman. Of seventy-six Senators in the Fifty-second Congress (omitting those from the six newly-admitted States[1]) forty have passed their first term. It has been often stated that the South honors her delegates by re-election more frequently than the North, but an analysis of the Fifty-second Congress shows that the percentages of the two sections do not vary greatly.

A fair majority of representatives are usually re-elected. A few attain a service of five or six terms, and the dean of the body can generally look back upon over twenty years of continuous life in the popular branch. Too often personal reasons, party exigencies, or a mistaken devotion to the sacred cause of rotation interfere.

In the smaller field of local American bodies, long tenure of office not seldom prevails, and New York can boast that the late Republican leader[2] of the Assembly had been for twenty-two years elected to that body, and had been six times Speaker. Against this we may set a small town in an adjoining county of Connecticut, where nearly every important citizen belonging to the dominant party had served in the legislature; or we may instance a certain district in Massachusetts, where four small towns furnish in rotation a representative; we can easily count up seven citizens from a single part of one of these towns who have in this way illustrated the great principle of rotation in office.

The initiative in legislation, in so far as revenue matters are concerned, has been conferred, with substantial unanimity,

---

[1] North Dakota, South Dakota, Montana, Washington, Idaho, Wyoming.
[2] James W. Husted.

on the lower branch. This house stands the nearest to the people. And of all questions, those which affect the pocket-book may be called the most vital to the citizens at large. In the Spanish Cortes, however, either house may take the initiative. Familiar instances of the primacy of the lower branch in this respect are the American House of Represent-atives, the House of Commons, the Danish Folkething, and the Portuguese Chamber. The Bundesrath, essentially a diplomatic body, and hardly furnishing a real parallel to other senates or conclaves of peers, is an apparent exception to the general rule; it originates bills, has an oversight of the administration, and possesses important confirming powers. Fourteen of its fifty-eight votes can negative a constitutional amendment. The restrictions laid on the upper house are exemplified in some constitutions. For instance, in the Netherlands, it cannot amend the bills of the lower body. but must accept or reject them *in toto*. The British House of Lords cannot amend a money bill, neither can the Cana-dian Senate. The upper house of the Prussian Landtag cannot amend the budget.

The relations to the executive show great divergence. Countries of the English type display the ministerial respon-sibility well developed. On the Continent generally the con-nection is somewhat slighter. In Sweden and Norway it is undefined. Affairs in Germany may be said to be in a somewhat anomalous position. To be sure, the German Constitution "creates no ministry responsible to the legis-lature."[1] But the system of government seems to be in a transition stage between the one-man rule of quasi abso-lutism under constitutional forms, and the liberal *régime* of modern times. There is no ministerial responsibility in Switzerland. Between the Anglo-Continental system and the Congressional plan there is, as was remarked above, a world-wide difference.

---

[1] Burgess, *Political Science*, II., 26.

The sovereign of a monarchy or the president of a republic still has, with few exceptions, some share—often considerable—in legislation.[1] The German emperor has vast power; the other European constitutional sovereigns generally less. The king of Sweden has an absolute veto in Sweden, and promulgates various laws, though in his office as king of Norway he has a suspensive veto only, and possesses some temporary powers when the Storthing is not sitting.

The restrictions placed on national governments by different constitutions are well illustrated in the United States and Canada. In the latter the Dominion Parliament has all powers not expressly conferred on the Provinces. The American States retain all powers not definitely bestowed on the Federal Congress. The wide field of legislation occupied by the Parliament at London is well contrasted with the narrower scope of our Congress. "Consider the most important subjects of legislation in England during the present century, the subjects which make up almost the entire constitutional history of England for eighty years. These subjects are: 'Catholic emancipation, parliamentary reform, the abolition of slavery, the amendment of the poor-laws, the reform of municipal corporations, the repeal of the corn laws, the admission of Jews to Parliament, the disestablishment of the Irish Church, the alteration of the Irish land laws, the establishment of national education, the introduction of the ballot, and the reform of the criminal law.' In the United States only two of these twelve great subjects could be dealt with by the Federal government, (repeal of the corn laws and the abolition of slavery). All the other questions enumerated would have to be dealt with by our State governments."[2] Important undertakings are now often authorized by private bills[3] in the British Parliament.

---

[1] The President of Honduras has the absolute veto.
[2] Fiske, *Civil Government*, 177.
[3] S. Walpole, *The Electorate and the Legislature*, 132.

As another instance of differing powers, the national legislature can—in Mexico for instance—determine the conditions of suffrage; in Germany, Canada, and Switzerland, it attends to details only;[1] and in the United states this matter is left to the separate States.

The centralized tendencies of the French system are too well known to require comment, although the provisions of the Constitution are, comparatively, neither numerous nor complex.[2] Our Congress plays a lesser part in legislation touching individual liberty, as that matter is provided for in the Constitution. In such powerful States as France, Germany, and Great Britain, legislation has a far greater share in establishing such civil liberty as exists.[3]

The Federal Assembly of Switzerland has elective and judicial powers. The House of Lords is a judicial body in impeachment matters, as is the American Senate; and the Storthing is also a high court of impeachment, in which the Lagthing and Odelsthing have parts analogous to those of our houses of Congress. The Bundesrath acts as a court in certain cases. The French National Assembly has the important duty of electing the President of the Republic, while the Swiss Federal Assembly chooses the entire executive (Federal Council).

The provinces covered respectively by organic law and statute law are loosely defined in many countries, Switzerland[4] for instance. Some recent State constitutions introduce provisions that older State constitutions have left to the discretion of the legislatures.[5]

Every parliamentary body has, of course, a presiding officer and such functionaries as clerks or secretaries, and doorkeepers, messengers or intermediaries between the different branches of government, and various attendants. The

---

[1] B. Moses, *Federal Government in Switzerland*, 99.

[2] Wilson, *State*, 200.

[3] Burgess, *Political Science*, I., 182, etc.

[4] McCracken, *Federal Government in Switzerland*.

[5] Fiske, *Civil Government*, 194.

Speaker—as he is usually styled in Anglo-Saxon countries, the President, to use his ordinary title elsewhere—is a personage of great importance. But in Great Britain his functions are those of a presiding officer principally, and this is usually the case. But British or colonial speakers, presidents of chambers of deputies, sink into comparative insignificance beside the American Speaker. This august personage has become in importance the second in the country. Member and a chief leader of the party in control of the House of Representatives, he appoints the committees which shape all legislation. Through the make-up of these committees he promotes or retards policies and measures of great moment. Interpreting with much latitude his functions as presiding officer, he recognizes on the floor those whom he selects. An interesting contrast is furnished between republican United States and monarchical Spain. In the former a new member, or one having no especial prominence, may for a session vainly try, though endowed with extraordinary lung-power, to " catch the Speaker's eye"; in the latter any member can hand his name in advance to the Speaker, who assigns to him a turn on the floor.[1] The vast appointive power of the Speaker is possessed on a smaller scale by the Speakers of the State legislatures.

The rules of the American House are much more complicated than those of the Senate. Indeed, so intricate are the House rules that one or two sessions must ordinarily be passed before a member is fairly well equipped for the business. As members not unfrequently serve but a term or two, this complexity of rules must have marked results on legislation. Certain days are set apart for particular branches of legislation, as in the House of Representatives, Monday for new bills on the roll call of the States, Friday for private bills, etc.;[2] in the House of Commons, for example, Mondays, Thursdays and Fridays are reserved for government orders, Tuesdays for notices of motions.

---

[1] *Cf. e. g.*, H. M. Field, *Old Spain and New*, 107.

[2] Wilson, *Congressional Government*, 73.

Intercourse between the chambers is conducted with less state than formerly. In cases of disagreement between the two houses, conference committees arrange a compromise; on this point a curious and perhaps praiseworthy provision exists in Austria: " if a disagreement arise between the chambers (of the Reichsrath) upon a question of finance or of military recruitment, the lowest figures or numbers are to be considered adopted." [1]

To facilitate legislation and check useless talking and obstruction, recourse is had to various devices. In the United States the previous question is used. Closure has been practiced in recent years in England as well as on the Continent, though one important British colony has not followed in the maternal footsteps.[2] A radical change in this respect was effected by the 51st Congress, in 1890, which adopted a new set of rules; the leading point of this celebrated code was the following: " The names of members (sufficient to make a quorum) in the hall of the House who do not vote shall be noted by the Clerk and recorded in the journal, and reported to the Speaker with the names of the members voting, and be counted and announced in determining the presence of a quorum to do business."[3]

As already hinted, committee government reaches its greatest development in the United States. There is a peculiar arrangement in France. The Senate has nine bureaux, and the Chamber has eleven. These select the committeemen monthly by lot. These committees are named: those on leave, petitions, parliamentary initiative, and local interests, and they consider propositions of private members; but financial matters are considered in the Senate by a special standing committee of eighteen members, the Finance Committee, and in the Chamber by a like body of thirty-three,

---

[1] Wilson, *State*, 347.
[2] No closure in the Dominion Parliament; Bourinot, *J. H. U. Studies*, 7th *series*, 572.
[3] 51st Congress. *Rules*, XV., 3.

the Budget Committee.[1] The German Reichstag has no standing committees,[2] but the Bundesrath has twelve. In Norway the Lagthing, comprising one-fourth of the Storthing, is itself a sort of revising committee. In Sweden there is a peculiar feature in the existence of a joint committee of the houses on legislation.

The Dominion Parliament has important committees on private bills, public accounts, agriculture and colonization. It has one colossal committee of 160 members on railways. These committees are appointed by a bureau called the committee of selection.[3]

This feature of a committee of selection is taken from the British House of Commons. That committee appoints the select committees, alone or in conjunction with the House, or the House alone may appoint them in some cases.[4] The Committee of Selection is itself appointed by the House.[5] The House has two standing committees on trade and legal affairs; on financial matters there are two committees of the whole House: the Committee of Supply—on the estimates— and the Committee of Ways and Means. In the Lords, the committees of the whole House, according to a recent reviewer, are the poorest, while the select committees do the best work.

Let us now take a glance at the elaborate committee organization of Congress. In the House of the 52nd Congress[6] there were forty-three standing and eight select. The membership ranges from 15 in the more important, like Ways and Means, to 7 (in the Committee on Expenditure in the Department of Agriculture). Far at the head of all in significance now stands the Ways and Means, appointment to which is regarded as nearly equivalent to the chairmanship

---

[1] Wilson, *State.*

[2] *Ibid*, 262.

[3] Bourinot, *J. H. U. Studies*, 7th *series*, 565, 569.

[4] S. Walpole, *Electorate and the Legislature*, 115.

[5] *Ibid.*

[6] 1891–93.

of an ordinary committee, while its chairman is sometimes affectedly styled the " Premier," from an erroneous analogy with the Chancellor of the Exchequer or First Lord of the Treasury. Among those of next consequence may be named, Appropriations, Judiciary, Interstate and Foreign Commerce, Rivers and Harbors, Elections, Banks and Currency, Coinage, Weights and Measures, Agriculture, Foreign Affairs, Military Affairs, Naval Affairs, Merchant Marine and Fisheries.

The Senate had forty-three standing and eleven select committees. The number of members on a committee ranges from eleven in the most important to three in the minor committees. Appropriations and Finance head the list, and then come Commerce, Foreign Relations, Judiciary, Interstate Commerce, Military Affairs, Naval Affairs, Privileges and Elections, Public Lands, Rules, and Fisheries, among the more important. The nature of the select committees may be inferred from such titles as, Transportation of Meat Products, Committee to Establish a University of the United States, Quadro-Centennial, Nicaraguan Claims, and Committee on President's Message Transmitting Report of Pacific Railway Commission.

To illustrate the character of the committee in a State body, let us take the make-up of the New York Legislature for 1891. There were 34 Senate Committees, of which the chief were: Finance, Judiciary, Railroads, Cities, Commerce and Navigation, Canals, Insurance, Taxation and Retrenchment, Miscellaneous Corporations. As illustrations of committees of a local nature, we may name those on Manufacture of Salt, and Game-Laws. The average membership of important committees was 7, on others 3. In the Assembly, Ways and Means, Judiciary, General Laws, Revision, Codes, Tax and Retrenchment, Canals, Affairs of Cities, Railroads, Commerce and Navigation, Insurance, Banks, and Excise head the list; while Soldiers' Home, Fisheries and Game and Indian Affairs serve to illustrate lines of legislation on distinctively local subjects. The membership of Assembly Committees was 11 or 9. Attention is called to the correspondence in names of the leading committees in the upper and lower houses and those in the two houses of Congress.

Now, to illustrate the use of committees in a local legislative body, let us take Brockton, Massachusetts, a manufacturing city of about 27,000 inhabitants, which graduated from the town meeting and selectmen form of administration some eleven years ago. There is[1] a board of 7 aldermen, one from each ward, and a board of 21 common councilmen, 3 from each ward. They are elected annually and receive no pay; the aldermen hold meetings weekly, the common councilmen ordinarily once in two weeks. There are twelve joint standing committees, with an average membership of 5, of which we may mention as specially important those on finance, claims, accounts, public property, water, fuel and street lights, fire, highways, sewerage and drainage. There are two standing committees of the common council on elections and returns, and on enrolled ordinances, and these also give name to two of the seven standing committees of aldermen; the remaining five are entrusted with police, licenses, health, state aid, and buildings. A tendency to elaboration of committee organization is observable generally in the United States. Even the new State of Washington finds necessary 38 standing committees in its Senate,[2] and 43 in its House.[3]

The phenomenon of a permanent committee between two sessions is observed in the Bundesrath with its eight commissions, and on a smaller scale in Uruguay, where a committee of Parliament sits from July to February in the place of the main body.

Sessions are annual, as is usually the case with Congress; or there are sessions at intervals through the year, as in Europe; or, as in nearly all the American States, the sessions are biennial; only five States, viz. New York, Massachusetts,

---

[1] *Brockton City Government,* 1889.
[2] More than one to each of the 35 members.
[3] *Legislative Manual of Washington,* 1891–92.

Rhode Island, New Jersey, and South Carolina, retain annual sessions, and those of Ohio are virtually annual.

The opening and closing of sessions take place with more or less of pomp and ceremony, with accompaniments of speeches from the throne and presidential messages, with important announcements, with unusual concourse of visitors, and frequent hurry and rush of measures, in the closing hours. The German Chancellor in his opening address to the Reichstag stands like a statue in full armor, leaning on his sword. In the Diet of Croatia and Slavonia the ceremonies of opening and closing are still "performed with a pomp and parade worthy of the Middle Ages."[1]

On the subject of parliamentary manners, an American, fresh from contemplation of proceedings in Congress or a State legislature, is inclined to think that turbulence is often the order of the day. The solemn carrying of the mace through the National House of Representatives is, however, a rare occurrence. Careful attention to the business of the house is uncommon in both branches of Congress, where members may be observed reading, writing or telling stories, and an orator sometimes speaks to a corporal's guard, while the vast majority fly to the cloak rooms.[2] With this habit we may compare the practice in the British House of Commons of "scraping down" a long-winded speaker. An inspection of the records two generations ago shows an advance. Imagine such a scene occurring now, even in a passionate debate, as took place in Jackson's time, between Randolph of Roanoke and a rough fighter from Connecticut, when personal allusions on mutual bodily infirmities were interchanged in language that cannot be reported, apparently without reprimand. But parliamentary good manners and orderliness are still far below the ideal. In the British House of Commons bear-garden scenes took place when Gladstone was assailed in 1885. One orator used the unrebuked

---

[1] Victor Tissot, *Unknown Hungary*, I., 117.

[2] *E. g.*, a Senator, well equipped on his theme, recently read his carefully prepared address to an audience of one.

euphemism " You are a liar." [1]   The *Saturday Review*, surely
no unfriendly critic on home matters, thus declares: " The
House of Commons hardly comes up any longer to the
recognized standard of a debate in Washington." [2]   In the
Italian Chamber of Deputies "the violent remarks of the
Socialist leader, Signor Cipriani, who was frequently called
to order, led to so great an uproar that the presiding officer
was obliged to suspend the sitting." [3]   Similar occurrences
happened in the French Chamber of Deputies in the winter
of 1891-92; " Unbridled license. prevails," [4] says one writer.
In a recent session of the lower house of the Austrian
Reichsrath the word traitor was used and was followed by
a scene of indescribable tumult; a crowd of Czechs sur-
rounded the orator, threatening physical violence, and the
presiding officer was forced to close the sitting. [5]

It is pleasant to note the testimony of observers in the
other direction. Thus an habitual attendant remarks that
" many years have passed since a member (of the Dominion
House of Commons) has been named and censured." [6]   The
courtesy and order in the Spanish Cortes have attracted
favorable attention. All State legislatures are not bear-
gardens. And we may believe that such scenes as those
above described are sporadic.

The personality of members is an important matter. And
we have now to consider the vocations and the general grade
of intelligence and ability. In this country lawyers lead;
bankers, merchants, manufacturers, business men in general,
farmers, and a sprinkling of doctors, professors, and clergymen is found. But the latter classes are rarely seen in
Congress. The 52nd Congress had only one or two examples of the " scholar in politics." Local conditions may

[1] *Fortnightly Review*, 45 : 264.

[2] *Saturday Review*, March 4, 1882.

[3] N. Y. *Herald* dispatch, Dec. 6, 1891.

[4] In 1889.

[5] N. Y. *Tribune*, Nov. 19, 1892.

[6] Bourinot, in *J. H. U. Studies*, 7th *series*, 572.

bring certain occupations to the front; as the farmers in many State legislatures. On the other hand, a great city's contingent to the legislature and the municipal body may present peculiar features. Witness the annual records of that Doomsday Book, the " Directory for Voters," published by the Reform Club of New York; in these ominous analyses the statements "liquor-dealer," "no ostensible business but politics," "practical politician," "lawyer of the lowest type," follow one another with tiresome regularity.

We may quote here a remark of an American publicist: "There is no country where so little respect is paid to acquirements, preparation, training in the arts of legislation and g vernment. Lawyers are generally preferred for such offices, it is true, but this is not because they are learned in the law, but because their vocation has given them readiness of speech ";[1] against this, we may set the recent prejudice against lawyers evinced by the Populists in Kansas.

The House of Commons is still recruited very largely from men of the leisure class. Younger sons of peers, lords by courtesy, knights, large land-owners, still figure prominently on the roll. But successful bankers, merchants and manufacturers are numerous. The "scholar in politics" is more largely represented than in the United States. Here as elsewhere the tendency manifested by men of the masses to be led by men of the classes, may recall to the student of general history the austere figure of Pericles, the hero of the demos, those blue-blooded aristocratic tribunes Tiberius Gracchus and Drusus, Mirabeau, and many others. The mass of the temporal peers is composed of scions of families who have appeared for ages in lists of the nobility or landed gentry. But the ranks are steadily recruited from new blood; a *novus homo*, a successful general, brewer, or poet, bureaucratic administrator, or treasury bench dignitary may look with some confidence to the time when he shall be gazetted to a viscountship or barony.

---

[1] H. White, *Fortnightly Review*, 1879.

The aristocratic *personnel* of the British Parliament is, naturally, not so marked in her colonial assemblies. The Parliament of Victoria contains a fair sprinkling of men from the ranks.[1] In a body of the composition of the House of Lords, absenteeism is common, and sneers at "hereditary legislators" and "drunken lords" or "sporting lords" are only too well founded. The regular business is in fact usually transacted by thirty or forty members. Yet it is shown that about three-fourths of the lords speak or vote each session. Journalists are popular candidates in France. In the same country a man of letters or a *savant*, a distinguished novelist, poet, historian or scholar has an ambition— often satisfied—to crown his career by election to the National Assembly. To a great degree the members of the lower house of the Spanish Cortes are educated men of position; and a recent cabinet in this monarchy, with its traditions of grandees and a proud nobility, did not contain a man with a title.[2] In Germany the "learned element" is probably present in fuller force than elsewhere. The Frankfort Parliament of 1848 was, as is well known, described as an assemblage of professors; and the same tendency is still visible to a less extent.

The average ability of legislators is a far more difficult problem. Flings at the United States Senate as a club of millionaires are common; and it must be said that there seems no immediate prospect of a return to the epoch of Webster, Clay and Calhoun; and it is undoubtedly true that a rich man, of slender equipment for legislative duties, can often reach this branch of Congress. But, it is urged, these Senators cannot be men of light calibre; amidst the fiercest competition they have forced their way to the front. The standard in State legislatures does not seem to be improving, if we may judge from recent indications.

---

[1] *Fortnightly Review*, 1879.
[2] H. M. Field, *Old Spain and New*, 107.

In local boards of aldermen and councilmen, the quality of a city's law-givers depends apparently on the size of the municipality, the indifference of a large mass of good citizens to their political duties, and the growth of rings. Bold indeed would be the man who would assert that New York City had not as large a proportion of virtuous and enlightened citizens as a small city in—let us say—Massachusetts. And bolder still would be the man who would institute a comparison between their respective city councils.

In England the popular conception is undoubtedly expressed by the saying when a talented Commoner has been translated to the Lords, that " he has been kicked upstairs." At a modern election (1870), according to a late publicist,[1] "a few Liberals of recognized ability stood for Parliament and failed, with a single exception in Scotland, because being men of limited means they could only afford to contest constituencies where the influence of great landlords predominated." And Hare points out that the decrease of rotten boroughs has caused fewer young men of marked ability to enter public life.[2] The days have nearly passed when a Pitt, Palmerston, or Gladstone can hold important offices or rise to prominence almost immediately after quitting the school or university. It has been observed that political scholars generally do better work outside of Parliament, as witness Bentham, Grote, Fonblanque, and Harrison.

A careful observer of Canadian affairs says: " The (Canadian) House of Commons comprises many of the ablest men of the country, trained in law and politics."[3] On the Continent it is supposed that the average ability and character of the elected bodies is quite high; and this would seem to be true in those countries where a large amount of self-government has been intelligently practiced. The French Senate, it is stated, will not suffer in comparison with the Chamber of Deputies.[4] The turbulence noted in

---

[1] *Fortnightly Review*, 1879.   [2] Thomas Hare, *Representatives.*
[3] Bourinot, *J. H. U. Studies,* 7th *series,* 561.
[4] Burgess, *Political Science*, II., 112.

some of these Continental bodies may be racial, rather than a criterion of character.   Sir Charles Dilke, than whom there are few more attentive observers of Continental politics, makes this unfavorable comment: "There is a little eccentricity in Italian politics, shown by the occasional return of swindlers, libellers, lunatics and murderers to sit at Montecitorio."[1]   Exceptions do not make the rule.   The Hungarians are natural politicians; "A candidate (for the Hungarian Reichstag) rarely spends less than £800 to warm his seat, and £8000 have been spent."[2]   The Spaniards crave a seat in the Cortes, and pay liberally for the privilege.

We next consider briefly the subject of local representative assemblies.   Passing over the familiar State and Territorial legislatures and municipal councils of this country, we find that in Spanish America local self-government is theoretically generally provided for.   Each State in Mexico has a legislature, popularly elected, as has Venezuela, whose government is quite decentralized.   Less liberal is the local government of Colombia and Bolivia.   Chili has popularly elected departmental municipalities.   Peru has a partial provision in this respect, with its Municipal Councils elected by provincial colleges, and Costa Rica has cantonal municipal government.[3]   In government as elsewhere, no two things are often farther apart than theory and practice, and the government of Guatemala, which enjoys universal suffrage, is stated by a late exhaustive writer on her present condition, to be "republican in name only."[4]   The large and progressive republics of Brazil and the Argentine Confederation have State legislatures.

Local legislative bodies now exist in England and Wales, since the creation of the County Councils in 1888.   For these purposes there is a division into 60 administrative counties, 61 county boroughs, and London, in all 122 districts.   Coun-

[1] Dilke, *Present Position of European Politics*, 230.
[2] Tissot, *Unknown Hungary*, II., 136.
[3] J. B. Calvo, *Costa Rica*, 161.
[4] W. T. Brigham, *Guatemala*, 321.

cillors are elected by popular vote for a term of three years. In turn the councillors elect aldermen who serve for six years, one-half retiring every three years. The councils are, however, subordinate to the Local Government Board of the central government. They legislate on the management of bridges, rates, hiring money, Parliamentary registration and polling districts; they manage certain asylums and reformatory schools, license halls for dancing, supervise the salaries of certain officers, etc. Except in London, they control the police, conjointly, however, with the justices of the peace. County Councils in Scotland, similar in most respects, were created in 1889. Ireland has no popular government in the counties.

The municipal corporations of England have councils, elected by rate-payers, whose term is three years; one-third of the councillors retire every year. These bodies possess wider powers than the county councils and have, in particular, a fuller control of police. The councillors elect the aldermen and mayor. The County Council for London is an important body of 128 members; the City of London has a close board of 25 aldermen. Popular municipal government in Scotland exists; in Ireland some of the towns are partially self-governing. The city government of such large British cities as Glasgow and Birmingham has attracted wide and favorable comment.

Canada has provincial Parliaments with large local powers. These Parliaments have two chambers, as in Quebec and the Maritime Provinces, or one chamber, as in Ontario, Manitoba and British Columbia. The North-West Territories have a Legislative Assembly, mostly elected. The local bodies in the small British colonies are partly elected, partly nominated. Local self-government in Australia is rather restricted. New Zealand has popularly elected county councils, and elsewhere there is popular government to a certain extent. The Cape, however, has quite a system of bodies below its Parliament, divisional councils, partially elected city councils, and Village Management Boards. In the largest possession of all, British India, the local government principle has been recently introduced to some extent, though Home Rule for the country at large is jealously denied. The larger Indian towns, and many of the smaller, now possess committees, a majority of whose members are chosen by the rate-payers, and the experiment, according to a recent political writer,[1] was working quite satisfactorily in the Central Provinces.

France gives to its outlying possessions what Great Britain denies—representation in the National Assembly. Algeria contributes 6 deputies, and the colonies 10. Each French department has an elected *conseil général*, having little powers, and the elected *conseils d'arrondissements* are also of minor importance. Each commune possesses, through choice by universal suffrage, a municipal council, whose powers it is the object of the Radicals to greatly increase. Algeria, besides representation at Paris, as above mentioned, has a Superior Council, which votes a budget, elected by provincial councils for the three provinces.

Each province in Spain has an annual parliament (*Diputacion Provincial*), and the communes have elected councils (*Ayuntamientos*) of 5 to 39 *Regidores*. Italy has also provincial parliaments and communal councils, and the communal electorate is somewhat less restricted than the electorate for Chamber of Deputies. A peculiarity in the Belgian provincial councils is the standing committee of 6 members, which attends to local finances in the intervals between the 15 days' sessions of the full council.[2] Communal councils, too, exist, but the electorate is restricted in all the bodies. In the Netherlands, Provincial States, elected for six years, legislate for the provinces and choose the upper house. Permanent committees, called Deputed States, form the executive. Communes have elected councils. The central government keeps a close connection with these local assemblies. Local self-government is not so extensive in

---

[1] *Fortnightly Review*, 1883, 45 : 243.

[2] *Cf.* the committee of the Bundesrath, mentioned above.

Norway as in Sweden, although the former is considered to be the more democratic country. Both have town and communal councils, and Sweden has provincial councils.

Great diversity exists in Germany in the powers of the local bodies, and there is no uniform system. There are town and city councils, diets of the circles (*Kreise*), and provincial *landtags* of the Prussian provinces; the last, highest in importance of territory and population, have limited powers. All the Swiss cantons have representative assemblies, except Uri, Unterwalden, Glarus, and Appenzell, which furnish—in their *Landesgemeinden*—familiar instances of pure democracy.[1] The *Landtags* of Austria-Hungary may be regarded as local bodies, and some of them (*e. g.* the Bohemian diet) as, in a sense, national bodies. Their composition is described in the table. Just as in some parts of Spanish America we often find liberal provisions on paper, and indifferent performances, so in Servia we observe local assemblies for counties, municipalities and communes.

Legislative Assemblies in Russia may be dismissed with almost the brevity of the celebrated chapter on the " Snakes of Ireland." Householders of the *mirs* compose the communal assemblies, and delegates of the *mirs* compose the cantonal assemblies. The district and provincial *Zemstvos* have certain powers, as have the municipal bodies; but centralizing tendencies have been still further developed by the changes of 1889 and 1890. Finland has a Parliament which meets every few years. It has restricted powers, and is formed from the four estates of nobles, clergy, burghers, and peasants. The local self-government of the Russian Baltic provinces, which had been largely in the hands of the German nobility, has been nearly abolished by changes of 1888-89.

While establishing for herself an entirely new National Parliament, Japan has also provided for prefectural (*i. e.* pro-

---

[1] See the interesting description of the proceedings of the Appenzell Landesgemeinde in Bayard Taylor, *Byways of Europe.*

vincial or departmental) and city assemblies, with restricted powers. But she has joined the commonwealth of constitutional nations too recently to allow of any deductions on her parliamentary government.

No treatment of representative bodies would be complete without a reference to the growth of the referendum and initiative.[1] These principles can be given in no better way than in the language of the Swiss Federal Constitution: "Federal laws shall be submitted for acceptance or rejection by the people, if the demand is made by 30,000 voters, or by 8 cantons. The same principle applies to federal resolutions which have a general application, and which are not of an urgent nature."[2] This is in federal legislation. All the cantons, except Fribourg, now have the referendum in cantonal legislation. It may be compulsory, or facultative, that is, contingent on certain requirements. But the initiative goes further. To quote again from the same instrument: "The Popular Initiative may be used when 50,000 Swiss voters present a petition for the enactment, the abolition, or the alteration of certain articles of the Federal Constitution." "Petitions may be presented in the form of general suggestions, or of unfinished bills."[3] Seventeen cantons have the initiative.[4] And the system just perfected in the canton of Ticino is considered particularly noteworthy.

Belgium is agitating the matter. There are indications of an increase of interest in the United States, as was evinced by a plank in the platform of the Populist party. California recently[5] called for a popular vote partaking of the

---

[1] "It would be rash to say that we ought to adopt the Swiss methods without modification, or that they would be applicable to all parts in the present state of the Union, but they are worthy of careful consideration."—J. M. Vincent, *State and Federal Government in Switzerland*, 129.

[2] *Swiss Constitution*, Art. 89.

[3] *Swiss Constitution*, Art. 121.

[4] In 1891.

[5] November, 1892.

nature of "initiative," asking that its legislature should be "instructed" on the question of choosing United States Senators by popular vote, and the "initiative" of the people declared in favor of this innovation. So eminent a publicist as Mr. Dicey has lately advocated the introduction of the referendum idea in Great Britain.[1] The results produced by a general introduction of these principles would be certainly momentous; perhaps, as some think, they would lead to the abolition of an upper chamber, perhaps to a more direct popular interest in matters of government. And, possibly, the methods which apparently work so well in a small country like Switzerland, would prove impracticable if adopted by the Great Powers.

Recapitulating the results of our rapid survey, we observe the great development of the responsible ministry principle, and the inter-dependence of the executive and legislative. We note a few cases—like the Storthing—where some judicial functions are taken by the assembly, thus controverting the dictum of Montesquieu, "Lorsque la puissance législative est réunie à la puissance exécutrice, il n'y a point de liberté."[2]

We see a prevailing tendency to bicameral assemblies, confirming the saying of Lieber, "it is a truly popular principle to insist on the protection of a legislature divided into two houses."[3] We mark the strongly exclusive character of the upper houses in Europe, and the insistence on property qualification, prevalent even in Anglo-Saxon offshoots from the home country.

We consider the privileges extended in many places to professional men, and the restrictions frequently placed on priests, and sometimes on government officials. But no survey can fail to disclose the fact that some of the regions where laws are most liberal for electors and candidates, are

---

[1] E. Dicey, *Contemporary Review*, April, 1890.
[2] *Esprit des Lois*, p. 143.
[3] Lieber, *Civil Liberty*, 194.

among the least shining examples of self-government.   Certain South American republics, Bulgaria, and Hayti, have —so to speak—an excellent legislative plant, but we will not look for political salvation to come from Caracas, Sofia, or Port-au-Prince.

A consideration of the intricate details of the existing legislative bodies, with the changes occurring thick and fast before our eyes as we write, would be an inviting but vastly perplexing field of research.   It might well demand the most painstaking observation of minutiæ and the broadest historic grasp.

TABLE

OF THE LARGER REPRESENTATIVE ASSEMBLIES: COMPRISING THOSE ABOVE THE
RANK OF PROVINCIAL, DEPARTMENTAL, COUNTY, OR CANTONAL BODIES ;
AND GIVING THE MEMBERSHIP, TERMS, AND REMARKS ON THE
QUALIFICATIONS AND ELECTORATE.

COUNTRY.	UPPER HOUSE.	LOWER HOUSE.	ELECTORATE.
UNITED STATES. Congress.	Senate 88, 6 yrs, 30 yrs of age.	House of Representatives 356, 2 yrs, 25 yrs of age.	Universal suffrage.
MAINE. Legislature.	Senate 31, 1 yr.	H. R. 151, 1 yr.	
NEW HAMPSHIRE. General Court.	S. 24, 1 yr.	H. R. 359,* 1 yr.	
VERMONT. General Assembly.	S. 30, 2 yrs.	H. R. 241, 2 yrs.	
MASSACHUSETTS. General Court.	S. 40, 1 yr.	H. R. 240, 1 yr.	
RHODE ISLAND. General Assembly.	S. 37, 1 yr.	H. R. 72, 1 yr.	
CONNECTICUT. General Assembly.	S. 21, 1 yr.	H. R. 252, 1 yr.	
NEW YORK. Legislature.	S. 32, 2 yrs.	Assembly 128, 1 yr.	
NEW JERSEY. Legislature.	S. 21, 1 yr.	General Assembly 60, 1 yr.	
PENNSYLVANIA. General Assembly.	S. 50, 4 yrs.	H. R. 201, 2 yrs.	
DELAWARE. General Assembly.	S. 9, 4 yrs.	H. R. 201, 2 yrs.	
MARYLAND. General Assembly.	S. 26, 4 yrs.	H. Delegates 84, 2 yrs.	
VIRGINIA. General Assembly.	S. 43, 4 yrs.	H. Delegates 132, 2 yrs.	
WEST VIRGINIA. Legislature.	S. 24, 4 yrs.	H. Delegates 65, 2 yrs.	
NORTH CAROLINA. General Assembly.	S. 50, 2 yrs.	H. R. 120, 2 yrs.	
SOUTH CAROLINA. General Assembly.	S. 32, 4 yrs.	H. R. 124, 2 yrs.	

* In 1892.

COUNTRY.	UPPER HOUSE.	LOWER HOUSE.	ELECTORATE.
GEORGIA. General Assembly.	S. 44, 4 yrs.	H. R. 175, 2 yrs.	
FLORIDA. Legislature.	S. 24, 4 yrs.	Assembly 53, 2 yrs.	
ALABAMA. General Assembly.	S. 33, 4 yrs.	H. R. 100, 2 yrs.	
MISSISSIPPI. Legislature.	S. 40, 4 yrs.	H. R. 120, 4 yrs.	
LOUISIANA. General Assembly.	S. 36, 4 yrs.	H. R. 98, 2 yrs.	
TEXAS. Legislature.	S. 32, 4 yrs.	H. R. 115, 2 yrs.	
ARKANSAS. General Assembly.	S. 31, 4 yrs.	H. R. 89, 2 yrs.	
TENNESSEE. General Assembly.	S. 33, 2 yrs.	H. R. 99, 2 yrs.	
KENTUCKY. Legislature.	S. 38, 4 yrs.	H. R. 100, 2 yrs.	
OHIO. General Assembly.	S. 37, 2 yrs.	H. R. 111, 2 yrs.	
INDIANA. General Assembly.	S. 50, 4 yrs.	H. R. 98, 2 yrs.	
ILLINOIS. General Assembly.	S. 52, 4 yrs.	H. R. 156, 2 yrs.	
MICHIGAN. Legislature,	S. 32, 2 yrs.	H. R. 100, 2 yrs.	
WISCONSIN. Legislature.	S. 33, 2 yrs.	Assembly 100, 1 yr.	
MINNESOTA. Legislature.	S. 54, 2 yrs.	H. R. 114, 1 yr.	
IOWA. General Assembly.	S. 50, 4 yrs.	H. R. 100, 2 yrs.	
MISSOURI. General Assembly.	S. 34, 4 yrs.	H. R. 138, 2 yrs.	
KANSAS. Legislature.	S. 25, 2 yrs.	H. R. 75, 1 yr.	
NEBRASKA. Legislature.	S. 30, 2 yrs.	H. R. 84, 2 yrs.	

COUNTRY.	UPPER HOUSE.	LOWER HOUSE.	ELECTORATE.
SOUTH DAKOTA. Leg. Assembly.	S. 45, 4 yrs.	H. R. 124, 2 yrs.	
NORTH DAKOTA. Leg. Assembly.	S. 30, 4 yrs.	H. R. 62, 2 yrs.	
MONTANA. Leg. Assembly.	S. 16, 4 yrs.	H. R. 55, 2 yrs.	
IDAHO. Legislature.	S. 18, 4 yrs.	H. R. 36, 2 yrs.	
WYOMING. Legislature.	S. 16, 4 yrs.	H. R. 33, 2 yrs.	
COLORADO. General Assembly.	S. 26, 4 yrs.	H. R. 49, 2 yrs.	
NEVADA. Legislature.	S. 18, 4 yrs.	Assembly 36, 2 yrs.	
CALIFORNIA. Legislature.	S. 40, 4 yrs.	Assembly 80, 2 yrs.	
OREGON. Leg. Assembly.	S. 30, 4 yrs.	H. R. 60, 2 yrs.	
WASHINGTON. Legislature.	S. 35, 4 yrs.	H. R. 70, 2 yrs.	
NEW MEXICO. Legislature.	Council 12, 2 yrs.	H. R. 24, 2 yrs.	
UTAH. General Assembly.	Council 12, 2 yrs.	H. R. 24, 2 yrs.	
ARIZONA. Legislature.	Council 12, 2 yrs.	H. R. 24, 2 yrs.	
OKLAHOMA. Legislature.	Council 13, 2 yrs.	H. R. 26, 2 yrs.*	
MEXICO. Congress.	Sen. 56, 2 yrs. 30 yrs old, and property qual.	House Rep. 227, 2 yrs. Property qual.	All respectable adults.
GUATEMALA. Nat. Assembly. One chamber.	52, 4 yrs.		Universal suffrage.
HONDURAS. Congress. One chamber.	37, 4 yrs.		Manhood suffrage.

* Universal suffrage is the rule throughout the States, in the sense that no property qualification or restrictive tax qualification is required (except in Delaware as above noted, and except for the nominal payment of a poll-tax in many States). Rhode Island was the last to abolish property qualification (in 1888). Various restrictions exist relating to illiteracy and length of residence, and criminals, idiots, and lunatics are excluded, as elsewhere.

COUNTRY.	UPPER HOUSE.	LOWER HOUSE.	ELECTORATE.
SALVADOR. Congress. One chamber.	70, 1 yr.		General suffrage.
NICARAGUA. Congress.	Sen. 18, 6 yrs.	House Rep. 21, 4 yrs.	Universal suffrage.
COSTA RICA. Chamber Rep. One chamber.	26, 4 yrs.		Those able to live respectably.
COLOMBIA. Congress.	Sen. 27, 6 yrs (also 6 members nominated by the president.)	House Rep. 66, 4 yrs.	Universal suffrage.
VENEZUELA. Congress.	Sen. 24, 4 yrs.	House Rep. 52, 4 yrs.	Universal suffrage.
ECUADOR. Congress.	Sen. 32, 4 yrs.	Chamber Dep. *ca.* 33, 2 yrs.	Roman Catholic adults, literate.
PERU. Congress.	Sen. *ca.* 40, 6 yrs. 35 yrs old, property qual.	House Rep. *ca.* 80, 6 yrs, property qual.	Indirect election.
BOLIVIA. Congress.	Sen. 16, 4 yrs.	Cham. Dep. 64, 4 yrs.	Universal suffrage.
CHILI. Congress.	Sen. 43, 6 yrs. Large property qual.	Chamber Dep. 126. 3 yrs. Property qual.	Property or income qual.
ARGENTINE CONFEDERATION. Congress.	Sen. 30, 9 yrs. 30 yrs old. Income qual.	House Dep. 86, 4 yrs. 25 yrs. old.	General suffrage.
URUGUAY. Parliament.	Sen. 19, 6 yrs.	House Rep. 53, 3 yrs.	Literate.
PARAGUAY. Congress.	Sen. *ca.* 30, 4 yrs.	Chamber Dep. *ca.* 55, 4 yrs.	Universal suffrage*
BRAZIL. Congress.	Sen. 63, 9 yrs. 35 yrs old.	Deputies 202, 3 yrs. Non-eligible are: clergy, state ministers, commanders.	Exclude illiterates, soldiers, members of certain monastic orders, etc.
HAYTI. Nat. Assembly.	Sen. 30, 6 yrs, nominated by the H. R.	House Rep. 50, 5 yrs.	Citizens having some vocation.
SANTO DOMINGO. Congress. One chamber.	22, 2 yrs.		Restricted.
GREAT BRITAIN. Parliament.	House of Lords 559, include hereditary peers, bishops, 28 Irish peers elected for life, 16 Scottish peers elected for one Parliament.	House of Commons 670, 7 yrs. 21 years old. Exclude clergymen of English, Scottish, Rom. Cath. church, and peers.	Exclude: government contractors, returning officers, sheriffs (also non-eligible for House of Commons). Limited property or income qual.

* Bourgade, *Paraguay.*

COUNTRY.	UPPER HOUSE.	LOWER HOUSE.	ELECTORATE.
CANADA. Parliament.	Sen. 80, life; 30 yrs old, large property qual.	House of Commons 215, 5 yrs.	Property or income qual.
NEW SOUTH WALES. Parliament.	Leg. Council, 67, life, nominated.	Leg. Assembly 141, 3 yrs.	Property qual.
VICTORIA. Parliament.	Leg. Council 48, 6 yrs. large property qual.	Leg. Assembly 95, 3 yrs, exclude clergymen.	Universal suffrage.
SOUTH AUSTRALIA. Parliament.	Leg. Council 24, 3 yrs, property qual.	House of Assem. 54, 3 yrs, exclude clergymen and judges.	General suffrage.
QUEENSLAND. Parliament.	Leg. Council 40, life, nominated.	Leg. Assembly 72, 5 yrs.	General suffrage, plural votes.
WEST AUSTRALIA. Legislature.	Leg. Council 15, nominated, property qual.	Assembly 30, 4 yrs, property qual.	Property qual.
TASMANIA. Parliament.	Leg. Council 18, 6 yrs.	House of Assembly 36, 3 yrs.	Property or income qual.
NEW ZEALAND. Gen. Assembly.	Leg. Council 41, life, nominated.	House Rep. 74, 3 yrs.	Property qual.
CAPE COLONY. Parliament.	Leg. Council 22, 7 yrs, property qual.	House of Assembly 76, 5 yrs.	Property or income qual.
FRANCE. Nat. Assembly.	Senate 300, 9 yrs. Election indirect. 75 elected for life.	Chamber Dep. 584, 4 yrs, 25 yrs old.	Universal suffrage.
SPAIN. Cortes.	Senate ca. 360, ex-officio, hereditary, nominated for life or elected by restricted bodies.	Chamber Dep. 431, 5 yrs.	Universal suffrage. 25 yrs old.
PORTUGAL. Cortes.	House of Peers ca. 162, hereditary, appointed for life, or indirectly elected.	Chamber Dep. 173, 4 yrs, property qual. or learned profession.	Small income qual. or heads of families.
ITALY. Parliament.	Senate 335, nominated for life, and princes.	Chamber Dep. 508, 5 yrs, 30 yrs old, exclude priests, government officials.	Small tax qual. or class qual.
BELGIUM. Chambers.	Senate 69, 8 yrs, 40 yrs old, tax qual.	Chamber Rep. 138, 4 yrs, 25 yrs old.	Tax qual.
NETHERLANDS. States-General.	First Chamber 50, 9 yrs, property or high official qual.	Second Chamber 100, 4 yrs, 30 yrs old.	23 yrs old, tax qual.
DENMARK. Rigsdag.	Landsthing 66, (12 nominated for life, 54 elected restricted. 8 yrs.)	Folkething 102, 3 yrs, 25 yrs old.	30 yrs old and personal qual.

COUNTRY.	UPPER HOUSE.	LOWER HOUSE.	ELECTORATE.
NORWAY. Storthing 3 yrs. 114 members, 30 yrs old, qual. of electorate.	Lagthing. one-fourth of the Storthing.	Odelsthing, three-fourths of the Storthing.	25 yrs old, property, income, or class qual.
SWEDEN. Parliament.	First Chamber 147, 9 yrs, 35 yrs old, property or income qual.	Second Chamber 228, 3 yrs, 25 yrs old, and qual. of electorate.	Property or tax qual.
GERMANY.	Bundesrath 58, appointed by the federal state governments for each session.	Reichstag 397, 5 yrs.	Universal suffrage. 25 yrs old.
PRUSSIA. Landtag.	Herrenhaus,*hereditary and life peers, nominated and elected by restricted bodies.	Chamber Dep. 432, 5 yrs, 30 yrs old, tax qual.	Indirect election, those eligible for municipal electorate, 3 classes, arranged by direct tax-payers.
BAVARIA. Landtag.	Cham. of Reichsräthe 71, hereditary and life.	Chamber Rep. 159, 6 yrs, 30 yrs old, tax qual.	25 yrs, tax qual.
WÜRTEMBERG. Landsstände.	Standesherren ca. 30, hereditary or nominated.	House Dep. 93, 6 yrs.	63 Dep. chosen by citizens, others by orders or ex-officio.
BADEN. Landtag.	Upper Chamber ca. 30-40, princes, hereditary, ex-officio, nominated or elected by nobility.	Second Chamber 63, 4 yrs.	Election indirect. Exclude paupers.
SAXONY. Landtag.	Upper Cham. ca. 50, hereditary, nominated, ex-officio, or elected by restricted classes.	Lower Chamber 80, 6 yrs.	Tax or property qual.

Minor German States: Hamburg, Bremen, and Lübeck have aristocratic Senates, and houses of Burgesses, the two former with restricted electorate. Mecklenburg-Schwerin and Mecklenburg-Strelitz have a feudal Landtag. Hesse and Saxe-Coburg-Gotha have Landtags of two houses, the others Landtags of a single house. Electorate is restricted by tax or other qualifications, or, as in Saxe-Weimar, where all the citizens have the franchise, they elect but part of the chamber. The single chambers vary in size from Reuss elder line (12) to Brunswick (46).

| **AUSTRIA-HUNGARY.** Delegations 120. | 60 from the Cisleithan Reichsrath, 60 from the Transleithan Reichstag, (20 from each of the Upper Houses, 40 from the Lower). Term 1 yr. | | |
| **AUSTRIA.** Cisleithan part of the monarchy. Reichsrath. | Herrenhaus 212, Nobles, prelates, nominated life members. | Abgeordneten-Haus 353, 6 yrs. | Election direct and indirect, 24 yrs old, property or individual qual. |

*310 members, in 1889.

COUNTRY.	UPPER HOUSE.	LOWER HOUSE.	ELECTORATE.
HUNGARY. Transleithan part of the monarchy. Reichstag.	House of Magnates 456, hereditary, life, prelates, dignitaries, delegates.	House Rep. 453, 5 yrs.	20 yrs old, income, individual or small tax qual.
CROWN LANDS OF AUSTRIA.	Unicameral Landtags, term 6 yrs; composed of large landowners, prelates, etc., and representatives of towns, communes and guilds. Electorate restricted to large landowners, members of guilds, direct tax-payers. Number of members in Landtags: Lower Austria 72, Upper Austria 50, Carinthia 37, Görz and Gradiska } 22, Tyrol 68, Moravia 100, Bukowina 31, Dalmatia 43, Salzburg 26, Styria 63, Carniola 37, Istria 33, Vorarlberg 21, Bohemia 242, Silesia 31, Galicia 151.		
RUMANIA. Assembly.	Sen. 120, 8 yrs, 40 yrs old, income qual., (8 bishops included).	Chamber Dep. 183, 4 yrs, 25 yrs old.	Indirect election. Tax qual.
SERVIA. Skupshtina. One chamber.		ca. 200 (?) (In part having university degrees). 30 yrs old. Term 3 yrs.	Indirect election. Tax qual.
BULGARIA. Sobranje. One chamber.		250 for Bulgaria proper, and ca. 100 for Eastern Rumelia. 3 yrs.	Manhood suffrage.
GREECE. Boulé. One chamber.		150, 4 yrs.	Manhood suffrage.
SWITZERLAND. Federal Assembly.	Council of States 44, 3 yrs.	National Council 147, 3 yrs, exclude clergymen.	Universal suffrage.

Swiss Cantons have representative Great Councils; but Uri, Unterwalden, Glarus, and Appenzell have assemblies of all the citizens (Landesgemeinden).

MONTENEGRO. Leg. Council. One body.	8 members; 4 nominated, 4 elected.		Arms-bearing population.
ANDORRA. Council. One body.	24, 4 yrs.		Heads of families.
FINLAND. Parliament.	4 estates: nobles, clergy, burghers, peasants. Convoked ca. once in 4 or 5 yrs.		
EGYPT.	Leg. Council.	Gen. Assembly.	
ORANGE FREE STATE. Volksraed. One chamber.	56, 4 yrs. Property qual.		Property qual. of whites.
SOUTH AFRICAN REPUBLIC.	First Volksraed of 24, 4 yrs. Restricted for aliens.	Second Volksraed* of 24, 4 yrs. Restricted for aliens	

* Constitutional Amendment of 1890.

COUNTRY.	UPPER HOUSE.	LOWER HOUSE.	ELECTORATE.
JAPAN. Parliament.	House of Peers *ca.* 300. Nobles elected by their orders, members elected by large tax-payers, nominated members. Term 7 yrs or life.	House Rep. 300, 4 yrs. Exclude various officials, priests, military and naval officers. 30 yrs old.	25 yrs old, tax qual.
HAWAII. Legislature.*	House of Nobles 24, 6 yrs.	House Rep. 24, 2 yrs.	Educational qual. and prop. qual. for House of Nobles.

* Prior to the revolution of January, 1893.